Orangutans!

An Animal Encyclopedia for Kids (Monkey Kingdom)

Children's Biological Science of Apes & Monkeys Books

PRODIGYWIZARD
BOOKS

LET'S LEARN SOME INTERESTING FACTS ABOUT ORANGUTANS!

Orangutans are the largest living arboreal animals! They spend most of their time in the forest canopy.

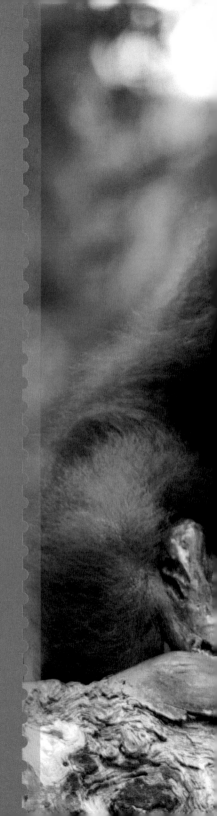

Orangutans are the only apes that lived in Asia. While others, like the chimpanzees and gorillas, lived in Africa.

In the wild, orangutans are
semi-solitary. They love
to be alone when they
reach maturity.

Female orangutans, in maturity, usually spend their time with their immature offsprings.

WHERE CAN YOU FIND THEM?

The first orangutans were found in Borneo and Northern Sumatra.

Over time, they were brought to Southern China, Indochina, Java and Southern Sumatra.

Nowadays, orangutans are extinct in all these regions. Like the gorillas, they also love to dwell in the trees.

Adult male orangutans love to climb up to the tree tops and usually spend 90 percent of their time in the canopy. They usually feed themselves with fruits and termites.

Female adult orangutans even love to stay in the treetops.

Over time, adult male orangutans will develop cheek pads. This will make their heads appear larger.

Once an orangutan gets his cheek pads, he will compete with other males in courting female orangutans.

His cheek pads also serve as an acoustic to project his long call to make others know that he is around.

Among other non-human mammals, orangutans have the most passionate relationship between mothers and their babies.

Mother orangutans will carry their babies for five years and suckle it for 6 to 7 years. The companion of the baby orangutan for the first eight years of its life is its mother.

The mother would sleep with the baby in the nest every night. Like humans, orangutans have 32 teeth. Orangutans are believed to be 7 times stronger than humans.

They are capable of traveling anywhere from 50 meters to 1,000 meters a day.

It is believed that their main predators are humans so they do not need a large social group to protect them.

In Borneo, Orangutans give birth once every eight years. Unlike other mammals, orangutans have the longest birth interval.

In Sumatra, they will give birth once every 10 years. They breed when they reach the age of 17 years.

As a result, if a female orangutan died, that would really affect their population and they would find it hard to recover.

WHICH IS HEAVIER? THE ADULT MALE ORANGUTAN? OR THE FEMALE ORANGUTAN.

The adult male orangutan is three times heavier than the adult female.

Although male orangutans are sometimes aggressive, orangutans are generally known to be gentle. They love to sit and gaze at their surroundings.

Like the chimpanzees and gorillas, the orangutans are notably smart. They are also capable of using tools.

Made in the USA
Las Vegas, NV
20 January 2021